MY CRAZY MY LOVE

"Sheer joyful gumption!... Fantastic, indeed. *My Crazy My Love* is less akin to a traditional (or even nontraditional) musical and more like the bewildering musical finale of the erstwhile Amazon series *Transparent*. In both cases, a standard family drama is turned upside down with singing and dancing... The result is a sort of vaudeville, DIY performance style... Make no mistake—there is a treasure trove of gems in this glorious mess of a show... The tone is something akin to a burning clown car on the side of the freeway... The penultimate, climactic scene sums up what's best about *My Crazy My Love*—a concoction of absurd humor, sharp wit with a dark edge, yet also containing real heartfelt sweetness and even a touch of wisdom... For those, like myself, who enjoy a messy, Fringe-y theatrical joyride now and again, this is definitely a show worth checking out. At the very least, it will make you feel better about your own family reunion."
—Michael Poandl, *Asheville Stages*

A "domestic phantasmagoria with song and dance," John Crutchfield's *My Crazy My Love,* set in a small, present-day Southern Appalachian town, in a sprawling house in condemnable disrepair, tells the raucous comic story of one family's failure to know itself. Only the impending death of the Finckelsteins' patriarch can offer some hope of eleventh-hour self-recognition and redemption. Or not.

Also published by The Sublime Theater & Press

American Arcade
by Steven Samuels

Washington Place
by David Brendan Hopes

MY CRAZY MY LOVE
*A Domestic Phantasmagoria
with Song and Dance*

JOHN CRUTCHFIELD

THE SUBLIME THEATER & PRESS
Asheville, NC

My Crazy My Love
Copyright © 2021 by John Crutchfield

Published by The Sublime Theater & Press, Inc.
49 Faircrest Road, Asheville, NC 28804-1848
ss@thesublimetheater.org

The Sublime Theater & Press, Inc. is a 501(c)(3) tax-exempt organization.

All rights reserved. Except for brief passages quoted in newspaper, magazine, radio, television, or online reviews, no part of this book may be reproduced in any form or by any means, electronic or mechanical, including photocopying or recording, or by an information storage and retrieval system, without permission in writing from the publisher.

Professionals and amateurs are hereby warned that this material, being fully protected under the Copyright Laws of the United States of America and all other countries of the Berne and Universal Copyright Conventions, is subject to a royalty. All rights including, but not limited to, professional, amateur, recording, motion picture, recitation, lecturing, public reading, radio and television broadcasting, online presentation, and the rights of translation into foreign languages, are expressly reserved. Particular emphasis is placed on the question of readings and all uses of this book by educational institutions. Inquiries concerning production rights for this play should be addressed to the publisher.

ISBN 978-1-952720-08-6 (Hardcover)
ISBN 978-1-952720-06-2 (Paperback)
ISBN 978-1-952720-07-9 (E-book)

First edition, May 2021

My Crazy My Love was first presented by The Sublime Theater at the BeBe Theatre, 20 Commerce Street, Asheville, NC, on November 7, 2019.

Written by John Crutchfield
Directed by Steven Samuels
Assistant Directed and Stage Managed by Rachel McCrain
Music by Holiday Childress
Choreography by Kristi DeVille
Set Design and Construction by John Crutchfield
Lighting Design by Steven Samuels and Rachel McCrain
Costume Design by Scott Fisher
Sound Design by Steven Samuels
Graphic Design by Art Moore

CAST
(in speaking order)
Archibald "Bub" Finckelstein…Steven Samuels
Julia Finckelstein…Kathy O'Connor
Randall Hodges…Julian Vorus
Kristin Finckelstein…Olivia Stuller
Kathryn Finckelstein…Emmaleigh Moriniti
Karen Finckelstein…Lydia Congdon
Scott McDowell…Art Moore

SETTING: The present; a small Southern Appalachian town; a sprawling house in condemnable disrepair, built with more visionary zeal than skill.

DRAMATIS PERSONAE:
ARCHIBALD "BUB" FINCKELSTEIN, about to turn 60. In a wheelchair. A native of Brooklyn and graduate of Harvard and Columbia Law School who "went native" in Southern Appalachia, married a shiksa, tried homesteading, failed. Is now the worst fiddle player who ever lived. Dying, but nobody knows of what.

JULIA FINCKELSTEIN, his wife, late fifties, a Southern Lady of sorts. Dreams of a Broadway career for her eldest daughter and a new kitchen for herself.

KRISTIN FINCKELSTEIN, their eldest daughter, late twenties, an aspiring yoga teacher. Tries a bit too hard to be a free spirit.

KAREN FINCKELSTEIN, their middle daughter, mid twenties, now in her last year at Columbia Law and on her way to becoming everything her father could have been and now despises: a successful corporate attorney.

KATHRYN FINCKELSTEIN, their youngest daughter, a teenage goth geek. Spends all her time reading Russian novels, writing in her journal, and recording songs on her laptop.

RANDALL HODGES, decent but schlumpy, early thirties, teaches Earth Science at the same middle school he himself attended. Has his heart set on marrying Kristin.

SCOTT McDOWELL, Randall's former best friend, early thirties, has made a fortune as an independent contractor in the fracking division of an energy conglomerate.

NOTES ON THE PLAY:

On the Set
As far as the actual set: maybe a jumble of dumpster-dive chairs, couches, stools, buckets, a wooden ladder, random defunct farm implements, a junkyard electric stove, etc.; everything at odd angles, nothing plumb or square; all necessary props and costumes buried somewhere in the detritus.

On the Actors
Unless otherwise noted, the actors remain onstage throughout the performance.

On the Music
Readers curious to learn more about the original music for the play should contact The Sublime Theater directly. While no musical scores exist for Holiday Childress's compositions, scratch recordings of the songs may be made available upon request. Nevertheless, it should be noted that future productions of the play are by no means obligated to use the original music, but are instead invited to set the lyrics to new compositions.

On This Thing Called Art
The characters and plot of the play are entirely fictional. In other words: the author made them up. Any apparent resemblance to actual people or events is a product of the reader's/audience's own creative genius.

MY CRAZY MY LOVE

Act One

OVERTURE

Lights flash up to an explosion of sound and movement, a cacophony of voices. The characters speak simultaneously as they move through the space, each arriving at some point down center to address the audience. The speeches repeat until all have had their moment.

BUB: Women! I'm surrounded by women! And every last one of them is completely crazy! "I need this, I want that, why don't you ever, why do you always!" Do I deserve this? Does anyone? No. No, no, no, no: God Is Dead and I might as well run off to Las Vegas, except I can't run off to Las Vegas or anywhere else for that matter, because these women are killing me!

JULIA: I've been asking for a new kitchen for twenty-five years. Twenty-five years! Can you believe it? Where did I go wrong? I'll tell you where. Falling for *that*. Archie never loved me. What he loves is Appalachian Culture! What does that even mean? The Dollar Store? The double-wide up the holler? Meth labs and gee-haw whimmy-diddles? Excuse me, but that is The Absence of Culture.

RANDALL: It was love at first sight. For me anyways. I know that's sort of a cliché and everything, but that's the way it was. We met at my friend Scott's wedding, at the reception. At the buffet, actually. She was getting a strawberry. Isn't that funny? She was standing there looking for just the right strawberry. And there was nothing else on her plate. And she was the most beautiful girl I'd ever seen.

KRISTIN: So like, I really don't need your negativity right now, OK? I mean, this is really stressful with Dad and stuff and having to be around them so much? I mean I want to be around them because I love them, but I also need time alone to get grounded and stuff, so like, all these questions? These questions and demands and criticisms? They really stress me out, OK? I'm trying to stay grounded and centered and like, joyful. And free! To be me! You see?

KATHRYN: Can you be in love with someone who doesn't exist? Is that crazy? I mean, it's one thing if they used to exist and you loved them and then they died but you still love them, because then they really did exist and you really did love them, except that now they don't exist anymore and the fact that you still love them is maybe a little awkward and embarrassing, since actually there is no "them" anymore to love, but whatever. But what if they never existed in the first place? Is that crazy?

KAREN: Idiots. All of them. Idiots and freaks. I hate them. And yes, by virtue of some cosmic insult, these freaks are my family. What am I even doing here? Oh yeah: Dad's dying. Of what? Probably disappointment. Because nobody believes in his hare-brained visions of rustic paradise. Songs about chickens. That's just great, Dad! Super! But you know, I think I'll just drive my brand-new Beemer all the way to the bank instead, OK? Enjoy your rancid cornpone!

SCOTT: Whoa! You see the rump on that filly? Knockin' me out, baby. Oh yeah! It's America, people, and I'm a goddamn American. Kickin' ass and takin' names. Rock and roll. Hit it and quit it. Hooweee! Hey, what's that awesome smell? Oh, shit! It's me! Can I really be this sexy? Hells to the yeah! Ever since I lost my beer gut and dyed my hair blond, you wouldn't believe the high-grade loin I been gettin'. I'm talkin' Grade A, USD. I'm talkin' turbo tang, yo. I shit you not. Florida does wonders for a guy. But hey, good to be back. For real now. The old hometown. Been away too long. So where's the party?

The whirlwind stops on a dime. Bub and Julia look at each other. Everyone else looks at them.

JULIA: You destroyed my life!

BUB: You had a life?

Beat. Another whirlwind, then stop. Randall and Kristin look at each other. Everyone else looks at them.

KRISTIN: I want…something…

RANDALL: Really? What? Maybe I've got it…here…somewhere…

Beat. Another whirlwind, then stop. Karen and Scott look at each other. Everyone else looks at them.

KAREN: And you are…?

SCOTT: What if I am?

Beat. Another whirlwind, then stop. Kathryn stands by herself. Everyone else looks at her. An awkward moment as she looks back at them.

KATHRYN: What.

Beat. Another whirlwind.

ALL: *(Chanting/singing)*
YOU ALL ARE FUCKING CRAZY!
COMPLETELY BATSHIT CRAZY!
YOU'RE MAKING ME FEEL CRAZY!
MY VISION'S GROWING HAZY!
MY BRAIN IS TURNING LAZY!
AM I THE ONE WHO'S CRAZY?
GOOD GOD! WHAT IF I'M CRAZY?
NOOOOOOOOOOOOOOOOOOOO!

IT'S YOU GUYS THAT ARE CRAZY!
COMPLETELY FUCKING
BATSHIT SUCKING
CONSUMMATELY CRAZY!

They stop in unison and stand there, embarrassed, avoiding each other's gaze, wandering off to various corners. Scott disappears behind his "glacier goggles." A strange music is heard.

SCENE ONE
A Strange Music

BUB: What's that strange music I'm hearing?

JULIA: I don't hear anything. Kids, do you hear anything?

Beat.

BUB: Oh. Well then it must be the private sound of angels come to whisk me away to Jesus. Here I am, fellas! Down here! That's right: the guy surrounded by unconscionable bitches!

SCENE TWO
The Girls at Sewanee

KRISTIN: Mom? Is Dad really dying?

KAREN: Sure smells like it.

JULIA: Oh, how can you even think such a thing? Your poor, dear, sweet Jewish atheist father, who sacrificed everything for us, even though he never really loved us! And now the medication is making him lose his mind! The final days of his life darkened by madness! It's unspeakable! Whatever shall we do without him?

KATHRYN: Return to Tara?

KRISTIN: Don't be sad, Mom! We're all like, totally here for you!

KAREN: Speak for yourself. I've got to go FaceTime with my stalker. You guys have fun! Or not! Whatever! I really don't care! *(Exits)*

KRISTIN: Why is she so hateful?

JULIA: She's just jealous, honey, because you're beautiful and perfect. Especially with that tight little yoga butt. Such a crispy little derrière, just like the girls at Sewanee, my alma mater.

KRISTIN: Thanks. Oh! I remember: can I have the credit card?

JULIA: *(Producing the card as if by magic)* Of course, sweetie! What for?

KRISTIN: I want to do this yoga teacher training retreat in Costa Rica for six weeks with Brad Superfine.

JULIA: Superfine? That's not a Jewish name, is it?

KRISTIN: Oh, my God! Mom, he's this like, totally super awesome famous yoga teacher! I've got all his YouTube videos on my Bookmarks Toolbar. And last year? In Carmel? At Brahmaputrid Institute? He totally invited me to come on this retreat with him!

KATHRYN: Just the two of you, eh.

KRISTIN: It's one-on-one teacher training!
(Vaguely tantric music. She sings. The others do the totally super awesome choreography)
We start out with sun salutations
To build up some heat in the core
Then practice our ujjayi breathing
To strengthen the deep pelvic floor

Then comes releasing the sacrum
As the serpents of Vishnu uncoil
And we partner to open the hip joints
While massaging each other with oil

Then it's Standing Pose, Lying Pose
So Good I'm Crying Pose
Horsy Pose, Froggy Pose
Snoop Doggy-Doggy Pose
Mussel Pose, Oyster Pose
Cleaving the Cloister Pose
Finishing off then
with Lotus Bloom Buttering
Butterfly Fluttering
Seventy-seven Times
High Up to Heaven Pose.
Ommmmm…whee!
Ommmmm…whee!

The music wafts away into the Indian Subcontinent.

KATHRYN: Right on.

JULIA: But haven't you already done your yoga teacher training, sweetie?

KRISTIN: Mom, you always need more yoga teacher training!

KATHRYN: It's kinda like psychotherapy.

JULIA: I see. And this Brad Superfine: is he single?

KRISTIN: Brad is totally like, free of all attachments and stuff.

JULIA: I'm so proud of you.

KRISTIN: I know.

They hug.

KATHRYN: But Dad's dying. You can't leave for six weeks while Dad's dying.

KRISTIN: Uh…*downer!*

KATHRYN: Plus, tomorrow's his birthday.

JULIA: Oh God! His birthday! I still have to bake the cake!

KRISTIN: Don't worry, Mom. It's not about the cake. It's about being together!

JULIA: No, sweetie, it's about the cake. Every year, he insists on a birthday cake. Just to torture me. He knows how I loathe to bake anything in that catastrophic oven, in that kitchen that is an offense to all decency. But he'll blister up with wrath if I fail to do so. You have no idea.

KATHRYN: Or maybe he just likes birthday cake. On his birthday. Kinda makes sense, right?

An awkward pause.

JULIA: Heavens! I am just sooooo tired! All this imminent death is just murder on my nerves! And the air is always so terribly damp in this house. It's hard to stay looking fresh! *(Exits with a flourish)*

KRISTIN: Look what you did.

KATHRYN: What.

KRISTIN: You totally like, hurt Mom's feelings!

KATHRYN: So?

KRISTIN: And you're not even sorry! God! *(Storms out)*

SCENE THREE
Fiddlesticks

The "man cave." Bub lies on his sickbed. Randall sits at his side. Something awkward has just happened. A long, uncomfortable pause.

BUB: You're serious.

RANDALL: Yes, sir.

BUB: You.

RANDALL: Yes, sir. Me. I thought you knew.

BUB: No, I didn't know. How the hell was I supposed to know? Nobody tells me anything.

RANDALL: I'm sorry, sir. I'm telling you now.

Beat.

BUB: Well, dammit!

RANDALL: Sir?

BUB: All I want in this muck-bucket of a life is a little hillbilly street cred. Holler cred, whatever. That's all I want. Is that too much to ask?

RANDALL: Um…I don't think I—

BUB: *(Overlapping)* And now my pseudo-hippie daughter finally gets engaged to a native, and what happens? He turns out to have all his teeth! What the hell?!

RANDALL: Begging your pardon, sir, but that is actually an offensive stereotype of Appalachian Americans. Oral hygiene has always been of particular—

BUB: *(Overlapping)* And you don't even have the accent!

RANDALL: The accent?

BUB: And why the fuck not, pray tell?

RANDALL: Oh. Um, I guess I just don't see any reason to wear it on my sleeve, sir.

BUB: And that's another thing: you've got sleeves! What about the overalls, no shirt? What about the, you know, the horny-toed clubfoot, for chrissakes?... I don't trust you. Go away.

RANDALL: Are you in a bad mood, sir?

BUB: Scram!

RANDALL: *(Rising to go)* As you wish, sir. But before I scram, let me just say I'm sorry the news of our engagement doesn't make you happy. I want you to know, however, that I have tremendous respect for you personally, and I assure you I will do my level best to be a good son-in-law. Moreover, I will love and care for your daughter as long as I live, and what little I earn as a middle school Science teacher will be hers for the asking. I only ask your blessing, sir. It can even be a provisional blessing, if you wish. *(Offers to shake hands)*

BUB: *(Eyeing the hand)* Wait a minute...

RANDALL: Sir?

BUB: *(Suspiciously)* You've got awfully long fingernails there...

RANDALL: Oh. Yes, sir. I play the, uh, the banjo, sir.

BUB: *(Slyly)* The banjo, huh...? And what's that got to do with anything?

RANDALL: Well, sir, that's the hand you use to strike the strings, see? It's called *frailing* or the, um, the *clawhammer* style, and it's sort of the traditional—

BUB: *(Overlapping)* Ha! I knew it! Oh, yes, I know all about the clawhammer style, boy, and don't you think I don't! Listen to you! Going on like you're talking to some know-nothing Yankee!

RANDALL: But you are a—I mean, you are from the North, sir.

BUB: And what if I am? What if I'm a Jew Boy from Brooklyn? You got a problem with that?

RANDALL: Oh no, sir, not at all. I was just explaining about the—

BUB: *(Overlapping)* Good. Because it just so happens that I *am* a Jew Boy from Brooklyn, and proud of it!

RANDALL: Yes, sir.

BUB: And my father was a Jew Boy from Brooklyn! And his father before that! And his father before that! And so on, back into the bog-like, pestilent prehistory of this great nation of ours!

RANDALL: Glad to hear it, sir.

Beat.

BUB: George Washington's insurance guy was a Finckelstein!

RANDALL: Really?

BUB: Little-known fact!

RANDALL: OK.

Beat.

BUB: So, how long you been playin'?

RANDALL: What? Oh, um, as long as I can remember, really. There was always music in our house.

BUB: Lucky you. Wish I could get one of these worthless wenches interested in it. But noooooo, it's all "Swaylor Tift" or "Bouncy" or some soulless hop-hip drivel. Hideous!

RANDALL: Right.

BUB: Where's the love in that music? Where's the humanity? Where's the *authenticity*?

RANDALL: I don't know how to answer that, sir.

BUB: No one does. Well, tell you what, kid: seeing as how we have so much in common, I may have a little job for you…

RANDALL: What job, sir?

BUB: Let's call it a role. In a little play I'm writing.

RANDALL: I'm not much of an actor, sir.

BUB: No worries. Luckily, I'm a dynamite director. But first things first, kid. Right now, I want you to go get your banjo, and maybe empty my bedpan while you're at it, and you and I will play us some bona-fide, straight-up, down-home, Smithsonian-authenticated, kick-butt, hillbilly fiddle tunes! How 'bout it?

RANDALL: You play the fiddle, sir?

BUB: Ha! Damn right I do, sonny boy. Watch this…
(Pulls a fiddle out from under his sheets, begins sawing at it horrifically. It's the sound of a thousand muskrats being skinned alive. Stopping abruptly, with genuine excitement)
Hey! Maybe I could play at the wedding!

SCENE FOUR
The Root Vegetable Chakra

KRISTIN: *(Sitting on her yoga mat in lotus position with her eyes closed)* Everybody feel the unique inner light of your spirit raining gently upon the mountaintops of your beautiful consciousness, like a soft breeze in the palate of life…yes…yes…remember to breathe…each breath is a unique blob of color in the watery flames of universal spirit and love and stuff and remember your intention that you set as your intention for your practice here today on this unique evening, and feel the root chakra connected to Mother Earth like where your iPhone connects when you charge it with an awesome flow of beautiful feminine goddess energy full of love and nourishment and sunshine on the foliage of your emotions, all of your wonderful emotions, aren't they just wonderful and true and sacred and unique, like pebbles on the shore with little bits of seashells mixed in and seaweed and the waves of enlightenment are washing up over everything like somebody's fanning you with a big pink feather, and now see if you can squeeze your perineum until you start to begin to feel a warm sensation of awesomeness rising up your—

KAREN: *(Off)* Hey doofus!

KRISTIN: *(Calling off)* I'm practicing!

KAREN: *(Off)* Practicing what?

KRISTIN: *(Calling off)* Uh: yoga!

KAREN: *(Off)* Yoga? What's that?

KRISTIN: *(Calling off)* Something beautiful and true that you'll never understand!

KAREN: *(Entering)* Cool. Can I watch?

KRISTIN: Um, I didn't give you permission to come into my room?

KAREN: This isn't your room anymore. It's the crafty room.

KRISTIN: It's still my room.

KAREN: Then where are all your 1980s Tom Cruise posters, bitch?

Beat.

KRISTIN: Will you just please go away, please?

KAREN: No, why?

KRISTIN: Because I really just need this time to myself? So I can practice my practice and get grounded and stuff, OK? I mean, maybe you hadn't noticed, but Dad's like, dying? And I need to be fully present.

KAREN: Fully present.

KRISTIN: Yeah.

KAREN: In the crafty room.

Beat.

KRISTIN: I totally forgive you for not understanding.

KAREN: Thanks. I owe you one. *(Beat)* Did you just fart?

KRISTIN: I love you SO MUCH!!!

SCENE FIVE
The Thorns of Life

Kathryn sits with headphones and electric guitar plugged into her laptop. She presses a button, records her song.

KATHRYN: *(Singing)*
I love you so much
It makes me wanna kill you
I love you so much
It makes me wanna die
You're kind of a dork
You're also kinda stupid
You're kind of a dweeb
Which makes you kinda fly—yeah!

I like the way you talk about mitosis
I like the way you slice up little frogs
I like the way you—
    (Messes up)
Fuck!
    (Hits the space bar, presses a few keys, resets the program, takes a deep breath, starts again)
I love you so much
It makes me wanna kill you
I love you so much
It makes me wanna die
    (Randall enters. At first she doesn't see him)
You're kind of a dork
You're also kinda stupid
You're kind of a—
    (Sees him, quickly hits the space bar, takes off her headphones, etc.)
Um…I'm trying to work here?

RANDALL: Sorry. Your mom needs us to go get some cake mix before the store closes.

KATHRYN: Why us?

RANDALL: Kristin's doing her yoga practice.

KATHRYN: Yeah. For the last three hours.

RANDALL: It's important to her.

KATHRYN: What about Karen?

RANDALL: Karen's, uh…she's had a bit too much to drink already.

KATHRYN: Perfect. What an awesome family. Maybe you should get out while you still can.

RANDALL: Plus, you're supposed to be working on your driving.

KATHRYN: I hate driving.

RANDALL: Fine. I'll drive.

KATHRYN: Score me some smokes?

RANDALL: Negative.

KATHRYN: Then at least let me ride double birdie.

RANDALL: Double birdie?

KATHRYN: Middle of the back seat. So I can flip people the double bird out the rear window.

RANDALL: Um, no.

KATHRYN: Why not?

RANDALL: Because I don't want to aggravate people for no reason.

KATHRYN: Are you afraid of conflict?

RANDALL: In a town where the average voting-age citizen is liable to pull out an AR-15 and blow you away at the slightest provocation? Yeah. Yeah, I guess you could say I'm a little afraid of conflict.

KATHRYN: Where's your AR-15?

RANDALL: My AR-15?

KATHRYN: Yeah. Don't you have one? The other guy has one.

RANDALL: I don't own any guns.

KATHRYN: Why not?

RANDALL: Because I'm not paranoid!

KATHRYN: But you're afraid?

RANDALL: Of conflict, yes. Which is why I avoid it.

KATHRYN: But what if you can't avoid it?

RANDALL: Usually I can.

KATHRYN: What if you can't?

RANDALL: That's a hypothetical situation.

KATHRYN: So what's your hypothesis?

RANDALL: Are you trying to piss me off?

KATHRYN: Yeah.

SCENE SIX
Vicarious Slappings

Julia, glass of red wine in hand, clears away trash from the kitchen so she can bake the cake. Karen slouches nearby, drinking straight from the bottle.

KAREN: Isn't that kinda personal, Mom?

JULIA: I know. I'm sorry. I'm just so curious to know what your life is like up there.

KAREN: Well, I can tell you, it's *Breakfast at Tiffany's* every day, Mom…

JULIA: Oh, when I got that internship at *Vogue*, I was the happiest girl at Sewanee! What a year that was! New York City!

KAREN: I'm glad somebody likes it.

JULIA: So much *culture*! So many opportunities to *interact* in a graceful manner, so many *occasions* to look absolutely *ravishing*! I could have lived there forever!

KAREN: Why didn't you stay?

JULIA: I wanted to! That was the whole point of marrying your father! I assumed we would live like royalty on the Upper West Side until the day we retired to Florida! But no sooner did he graduate Columbia Law than he took an advance on his inheritance and bought three thousand acres of snake-infested Lunsford County wilderness! *Why,* you ask?

KAREN: No, actually. I don't.

JULIA: Well, I'll tell you. This half-baked back-to-nature bunk about homesteading in Southern Appalachia! *As if!* He can't even hammer a nail straight! *After thirty years of trying!* Look at this place! And, oh God, since you left for school, he's grown worse and worse. He's started fancying himself some sort of backwoods Mozart or something. I've tried everything! Burning his fiddle. Pounding it into pulp and mixing it with his morning oatmeal. In vain. He must have a dealer. Oh, if only I had—

KAREN: *(Overlapping)* If only you had married Dave Blankenship, I know, Mom.

JULIA: *(Wistfully)* Dave Blankenship…

KAREN: Do we have any more wine?

JULIA: But we were talking about your sex life. So this fellow with the Lamborghini. What I just *have* to ask is—

KAREN: Jesus, Mom. Are you doing OK?

JULIA: What makes you ask that, honey?

KAREN: Well—

JULIA: *(Overlapping)* Because now that you mention it, no. I am not doing OK. How could I be doing OK? Your father has completely ruined my life and destroyed all hope of happiness.

KAREN: Well, but besides that.

JULIA: And now it appears he's going to die without even begging forgiveness!

KAREN: Katie says she thinks he's planning something for his birthday.

JULIA: He's always planning something. Some new way to humiliate me.

KAREN: Maybe he's planning to tie us all up and give a fiddle concert.

JULIA: An apt metaphor for my marriage.

KAREN: Why not take a lover, then? You still look good. In the right outfit.

JULIA: Am I some kind of cheap floozy? I'd rather suffer in dignified silence.

KAREN: Sounds like a really great plan.

JULIA: And by the way, what do you think of your sister's getting engaged to Mr. Schlumpy? Isn't it just…scandalous?

KAREN: Well, at least he has a job.

JULIA: But she deserves so much better!

KAREN: Really?

JULIA: Of course! She's perfect! And beautiful! Why isn't she a Broadway star?

KAREN: Um…maybe because she doesn't have any talent?

JULIA: What does that have to do with it?

KAREN: Good point.

JULIA: Having talent is for ugly people.

KAREN: You know, I've always wondered what it was for.

JULIA: I just don't like him. He's, well, *schlumpy,* for starters. And sneaky too. Did you know he's been living in our basement for the past four years?

KAREN: Yes, Mom. He's been renting from you.

JULIA: Well, the whole thing's news to me. A schlump living in the basement! Even if he is paying rent! It's positively *vulgar!*

KAREN: What it is, is pathetic. He's so in love with Kristin, he's willing to like, actually physically *dwell* in that mildew-furred shithole, while she breezes off to California to go "find herself," whatever that means, and like, what does he even *do* down there anyway? Slobber over her high school yearbooks? Fondle her moth-eaten tutus? God! I just hope Dad's old videos of her Junior Miss North Carolina tryouts aren't still down there. That one-piece you made for her was cut way, way, *way* too—

JULIA: *(Overlapping)* All of a sudden I've grown weary of this topic. Can we get back to Mr. Lamborghini? So…seriously, now, and I want to know the whole story: did he ever…you know…?

Beat.

KAREN: Don't you guys at least have some, I don't know, cough syrup somewhere?

SCENE SEVEN
The Postmodern Sublime

Kathryn and Randall stand in line at the grocery checkout. Randall is holding a box of cake mix. An announcement is heard in a creepy English accent.

ANNOUNCEMENT: Greetings, EarthLife shoppers! The hot bar will be closing in fifteen minutes. If you want anything hot from the hot bar you'd better get it right away. While it's hot. Oh yes, hot hot hot. You know it, baby. Hot! I'll be waiting for you…

KATHRYN: I totally want to lose my virginity to that guy.

RANDALL: God, I hate this place.

KATHRYN: What's there to hate?

RANDALL: This bullshit! I mean: "Organic." "Sustainable." "Fair trade." It's all corporate agribusiness now. Who do they think they're fooling?

KATHRYN: Nobody. That's the joke.

RANDALL: Seven dollars for a box of friggin' *cake mix*?

KATHRYN: And we're buying it anyway. Isn't that hilarious?

RANDALL: It's obscene.

KATHRYN: Dude, I hope you don't think my sister's going to let you shop at Kroger's.

RANDALL: Mung bean sprouts are just as good at Kroger's as they are anywhere else. Besides—

SCOTT: *(Popping out from behind them, a six-pack of local craft beer in each hand)* Home slice! I totally thought that was you!

RANDALL: Uh…Scott? Holy shit.

SCOTT: Yeah, bro! In da house! Reunion tour! Stylin' and profilin'!

RANDALL: Wow.

SCOTT: Wow-issimo, yo! You know it! So how's your hammer hangin', homes? Haven't seen you since I moved to Florida and got rich! Damn, you look old.

RANDALL: Thanks.

SCOTT: Just kiddin'. And who might this be?

RANDALL: Oh, uh, hey: this is Katie. Katie, this is Scott, uh, Scott McDowell. Scott's an old buddy of mine.

KATHRYN: Hi.

SCOTT: *(Sizing her up with a glance)* Damn, bro: goin' for the goth jailbait, huh?

RANDALL: Um, well actually—

SCOTT: *(Overlapping)* Hey, whatever keeps Mr. Happy happy, you know? Plus, I'm one to talk! Ha! But look, I like, totally just rolled into town, bro! Big fracking job up here, who'd a thunk it!

RANDALL: Fracking?

SCOTT: Yeah, dude! "Hydraulic fracturing." Good times, great oldies, and mondo moolah. Which reminds me: check it *(Pulls out his wallet)*: two grand in twenties, bro! And a ton of great ideas! So like, where's the hometown action these days?

RANDALL: Well, but isn't Jennifer—? I mean—

SCOTT: Shit, homes! Jennifer who? I'm single again! Didn't you hear? Mr. One-Track is Back! Yeah! So, like— Hang on, that's my cell. *(Looks at the number)* Damn. OK, so tonight: tequila shots and Putt-Putt? Bro-on-bro catch-up time!

RANDALL: Um, well…actually, I—

SCOTT: Done. *(Into phone)* Hey, baby! Yeah, so I'm up here… yeah… What're you doin'?… Yeah?… *(Winks at them, then turns away to finish his conversation, exiting)*

KATHRYN: What a studmuffin.

RANDALL: What is wrong with this cashier? Is she friggin' *tranquilized*?

SCENE EIGHT
The Dark Night of the Soul

Bub sits in his wheelchair in the yard. It is night.

BUB: *(Praying)* OK, Jesus: I know you're probably mad at me for being an atheist. I don't entirely blame you. Even though, when it comes right down to it, you've got to admit I've been a pretty damn good Christian for a Jewish atheist. But whatever. That's not what I wanted to talk about. Actually, I need to ask you a favor. Yeah, I know: "what right," yadda, yadda. But the thing is, Jesus, as of this very evening, I've got the final piece in place. My master plan! My magnum opus! My little existential swan dive into glory! It's really gonna happen this time. All I need, Jesus, is for you to promise me you'll keep out of it. Seriously. None of this divine intervention crap, got it? *Deus ex machina.* I mean it. Are we cool? Just keep right on acting like you don't exist. No matter what happens. And things are gonna get weird, believe me. Real weird. I'm talkin' old-school apocalyptic. Fire and brimstone, war and pestilence, the earth opening up, all that shit. But it'll be so worth it. I'm gonna leave these people something to think about for a long, long time. Oh, yes. My last birthday. And I'm gonna go out in style, goddammit! Now we're gonna see who's serious! Now we're gonna see who understands *legacy*! Watch and learn, boys! *Mazel tov* to me! *(Spins a "donut" in his wheelchair)*

SCENE NINE
The Lovers

Kristin and Randall sit together on the front steps.

KRISTIN: Oh my God—what is he doing out there?

RANDALL: I think he's just, uh, talking to himself or…something.

KRISTIN: He's getting worse and worse. This morning? When I was doing my morning practice? I could hear him playing his fiddle. It sounded like some little animal was being skinned alive. Like a bunny or something.

RANDALL: Yeah, it takes a while to sound good on the fiddle.

KRISTIN: I'm so afraid he's gonna do something like, really drastic and terrible?

RANDALL: Don't worry, honey. I think he's just a little wound up with everybody back home all of a sudden.

   Beat.

KRISTIN: Yeah, um, and could you maybe not call me that?

RANDALL: What.

KRISTIN: Honey?

RANDALL: What.

KRISTIN: No, I mean could you maybe not call me "honey?"

RANDALL: But…we've always called each other "honey."

KRISTIN: Yeah, but I don't care for it? I mean, honey is actually really really bad for you. It has like, a totally high glycemic index.

RANDALL: Oh. Um… OK…

KRISTIN: And also? Could you not follow me around so much? I've been meaning to tell you.

RANDALL: Do I follow you around?

KRISTIN: Um…yeah. Pretty much like, everywhere I go.

RANDALL: Oh. Well, I guess I've just really missed you, hon— ah, sweetheart. I mean, when you left for California, you said you'd be back in two years and we could get married. And, um, it's been four years now.

KRISTIN: Yeah, but you've been living in my parents' basement all that time? Which kind of freaks me out? I mean isn't that a little like, clingy and stuff?

RANDALL: Huh. I guess I just saw it as being part of the family.

KRISTIN: But you're not part of the family. I mean, you're not even Jewish.

RANDALL: Well, but we're engaged, so I sort of—

KRISTIN: And also? I sort of wish you'd stop pressuring me about that?

RANDALL: Am I pressuring you?

KRISTIN: I totally feel pressured. And I really don't need that right now. I mean, my Dad's dying? Which is why—

RANDALL: *(Overlapping)* I know, I know, which is why you moved to California in the first place. To study yoga and find yourself so you'd be emotionally and spiritually centered and prepared for this difficult time. I understood that. I supported it. We've all had to prepare ourselves.

KRISTIN: Yeah, but you're not being very supportive right now.

RANDALL: I'm not?

KRISTIN: No. You're pressuring me about the M-word.

RANDALL: But I've hardly mentioned it!

KRISTIN: Yeah, but I can feel you thinking about it? I mean, that's the amazing thing about yoga? I can totally feel your aura, and how clingy you are, and all the like, expectations and stuff.

RANDALL: But I'm completely in love with you, Kristin! I can't help it! And I love your family! That's why I moved into the basement!

KRISTIN: Um, they don't even know who you are.

RANDALL: Huh. Yeah, I guess I've noticed that. Which kind of confuses me. I mean, do they think *elves* bring in the firewood and shovel the snow from the driveway?

KRISTIN: And you're not even Jewish.

RANDALL: Why do you keep saying that?

KRISTIN: Because it's true.

RANDALL: I know I'm not Jewish. I've never pretended to be Jewish. I don't even—

KRISTIN: Well, but that's sort of a problem for me.

RANDALL: Really? But hon—. Kristin, you're not Jewish either, technically. I mean, your mother's a WASP if there ever was one.

KRISTIN: Um, I don't want to argue with you? This is what you always do.

RANDALL: I'm just trying to understand what you're talking about!

KRISTIN: Well, but I think that with Dad like, dying and stuff, it's important for me to think about my heritage.

RANDALL: Your—? OK…

KRISTIN: You know?

RANDALL: Sure, sure. Heritage. Right. So, um…what are you saying?

KRISTIN: I just think we should maybe sort of undo the engagement for now. Have like, a disengagement.

Beat.

RANDALL: Wow…

KRISTIN: I mean, you can still hang around and stuff, if you want to.

RANDALL: Well, I do live here.

KRISTIN: Yeah, so like I'm saying, you can hang around and help out and clean Dad's poop bucket and stuff, which is really sweet of you, but I'm going to kind of ignore you from now on, OK?

Beat.

RANDALL: That's not very nice.

KRISTIN: See? You're so judgmental! God! *(Storms out)*

Music: a cheerful children's melody set to a waltz. Karen does a burlesque routine for Randall's "benefit."

KAREN: *(Singing)*
O Love, it is so beautiful
O Love, it is so fine
It makes me feel like all the world
Is just as good as mine

O Love, it's like, so awesome—wow!
O Love, it's like, so great!
And if it shows up here at all
It's O so worth the wait!

O Love, it is so sparkly
Just like a brand-new bike
Except it's free and self-propelled
And lasts forever—*psych*!

The song winds up to a cheerful finale.

Act Two

Act Two

SCENE TEN
Kitchen Patrol

Julia and Kathryn are washing dishes.

JULIA: It's just so wonderful having my daughters here again.

KATHRYN: Um…I've been here the whole time, Mom.

JULIA: Karen is so smart and successful, and just looking at Kristin's butt fills me with hope.

KATHRYN: Me too.

JULIA: They're both such amazing people. I'm so lucky! The luckiest mother in the world.

KATHRYN: *(Simultaneously)* "The luckiest mother in the world."

JULIA: What would I do without them? Stuck in this awful dump with no one between me and that homunculus I had the misfortune of marrying.

KATHRYN: So why did you marry Dad, actually? I mean, I assume it wasn't for his looks.

JULIA: Well, that's where you're wrong. You may find this hard to believe, but forty years ago, Archibald Finckelstein was the handsomest man in North America. And alas for me, he was also a consummate seducer of Innocent Young Southern Belles!

KATHRYN: He seduced you?

JULIA: And all of my friends!

KATHRYN: Way to go, Dad!

JULIA: But with me he got more than he bargained for.

KATHRYN: You got pregnant?

JULIA: I most certainly did. Of which fact I promptly, like a dutiful Southern daughter, informed my Daddy, who at that time was a close personal friend of Major Winslow Goodwin Pratt, Founder and President for Life of the Shelby County Shotgun Club. He paid your father a little visit.

KATHRYN: A shotgun wedding, huh?

JULIA: But what a little fool I was! Instead I should have run away to, to, to Canada! to Mozambique! to—anywhere! Anywhere but marriage to that Semitic Dorian Gray! I wasn't even really all that pregnant!

KATHRYN: Wow.

JULIA: And my mother warned me. Oh did she ever. I can hear the old bitch now: "Marry whom you will, Julia, just so long as it isn't that Jew from Jersey City!"

KATHRYN: I thought he was from Brooklyn.

JULIA: Brooklyn, Jersey City. It's all the same.

KATHRYN: Right.

JULIA: Well, he got what he wanted.

KATHRYN: And what was that?

JULIA: Why, the sweet pastures of my virginal white flesh in which to sow the seed of Abraham!

KATHRYN: You were a virgin?

JULIA: Naturally!

KATHRYN: OK.

JULIA: But that's the way of these Semitic peoples. You don't realize it at first. They come with their flatteries, their glittering trinkets, they seduce you with their cabalistic eloquence, and then? They spite you for being seduced! Can you imagine anything more evil? Can you imagine a more cruel fate for a bright-eyed Southern Belle?

KATHRYN: Yeah, actually.

JULIA: Once I had the world at my delicately shaped feet! Now I have linoleum tiles! And most of them are peeling up at the edges, like the scales of some diseased iguana! It's hideous! But do you hear me complain? No. No, I shall remain poised and cheerful to the end. It's called breeding.

Beat.

KATHRYN: So did you and Dad never love each other at all?

Music: third-rate early 60s folk.

JULIA: *(Singing)*
How can you ask such a question?
Oh how can you be so cruel?
I loved him the moment I saw him
Sipping gin at the Dinglemann's pool.

And it was hot, oh yes
That summer was a doozy
It was hot, oh yes
Enough to make you woozy

He was dapper and chipper and charming
With a mischievous glint to his eye
And a suit I would swear was Armani,
With a Phi Beta pin in his tie.

And it was hot, oh yes
That summer was a doozy
It was hot, oh yes
Enough to make you woozy

But the moment that made my heart quiver
And I knew I belonged just to him
Was the moment he took my hand lightly
And said, Miss, shall we go for a swim?

And it was hot, oh yes
That summer was a doozy
It was hot, oh yes
Enough to make you woozy.

The song fades away.

KATHRYN: Wait. You fell in love because he asked you to go swimming?

The song starts up again.

JULIA: *(Singing)*
Oh I know that sounds silly and childish
But such are the ways of true love

A moment—it takes but a moment
And a soft slant of light from above.

And it was hot, oh yes
That summer was a doozy
It was hot, oh yes
Enough to make you woozy.

The song fades away again.

KATHRYN: OK. I guess I have to accept that. So then what happened?

JULIA: What do you mean?

KATHRYN: I mean: what happened? He was the love of your life and now you hate each other's entrails? I don't get it.

Julia sighs in exasperation. The song starts up again. Julia is about to start singing, but suddenly interrupts herself.

JULIA: Wait a minute. Who are you again?

KATHRYN: Um, Kathryn?

JULIA: Who?

KATHRYN: Your daughter?

JULIA: Which daughter?

KATHRYN: The one about to graduate high school?

JULIA: *(Remembering)* Oh… Right. That one. I keep forgetting.

KATHRYN: Yeah.

Beat.

JULIA: I'm sorry: what was the question?

SCENE ELEVEN
De Amicitia

A Putt-Putt golf course. Night. Randall and Scott play a round. Scott swings the club like he's driving a 300-yarder. Randall putts like a graduate student in the academic field formerly known as Library Science. A case of beer is close at hand.

SCOTT: Dude, and then, so like, I'm sittin' there, and the guy basically starts begging me not to steal his girlfriend and so forth, and I'm like, Hey, it's her choice, right? I mean it's a free country. It's a free market, right? Consumer is king. And believe you me, this chick's a *consumer,* alright? I'm mean, she can do some serious goddamn *consuming,* you know what I'm sayin'? Anyway, and so I'm like, Dave, bro, if she wants to shimmy up and down the McMeat Pole, who am I to stop her? Plus, and here's the thing, it's kinda like my duty, right? I mean, the haves and the have-nots and so forth. Open and shut. Anyway, and so the sob story, right? "I'll give you a promotion, I'll make you a partner, just please don't blah blah, she's the most important blah blah, she means everything to blah blah, I know it sounds crazy but blah blah," and the whole time I'm thinking, Shit, she's strappin' herself into the suit like, *right now,* waitin' for me to get over there, and I'm havin' to listen to this pathetic bullshit and so forth? And so I'm like, Dave, Dave, pull yourself together, bro. I've got a few more things I want to do to her, and then she's all yours again, OK? You can have her back. And he's like, Thank you, Scott! Thank you! What a great friend you are. And I'm like, Hey man: You're Welcome.
  (Randall loses)
Two out of three?

SCENE TWELVE
Are You There, Fyodor?

KATHRYN: *(Sitting in her room, typing on her laptop)* Dear Raskolnikov. I'm writing to break up with you. I know you'll take it hard, but that's the way it's gotta be for now. I've realized it's not fair to lead you on. I mean, I don't even know what love is. I think it might be a mental illness. The evidence is kind of pointing that way. Which sucks, because it means if I want to get laid by an actual person, I'll have to either go temporarily insane or else just do it in cold blood. Kind of the way you killed the nasty old bitch. By the way, I'm turning seventeen tomorrow, the same day Dad's turning sixty. It's weird having a birthday on the same day as your Dad, because the question always arises of whose Special Day it really is. Except that actually the question never arises. It's all about Dad. The whole family is about Dad. I guess it's no surprise I don't know what love is. OK, I'm bored.

She closes her computer, picks up her novel, puts in her earphones. We hear her evil music...

SCENE THIRTEEN
Know Thyself, Dammit

Julia sits at a small writing desk, a cocktail within arm's reach. In front of her is a preposterous gilt-leather bound journal, and a silver inkwell and quill. The worst imaginable sentimental 19th century orchestral music is heard from somewhere—maybe a small iPod player.

JULIA: *(Writing)* Dear Diary. Finally! A moment to myself. *(Beat)* All my hopes are dashed, and my dreams are but a crispy nub at the bottom of the toaster. Oh, if only I had married Dave Blankenship instead of that toad! Then I would be queen of a vast Floridian empire! But no, 'twas not to be. The Fates decreed against it. Nevertheless, I shall endure unto the bitter end. Which hopefully won't be much longer. And then I shall be free! Nevermore confined to this unspeakable dungeon of a house! Nevermore to waste my charms in the stinky wilderness! But the end won't be easy. Already, the enemy is growing more violent in his ravings. Let us hope these are the immediate precursors to his death throes. But whatever evil he may yet wreak, at least I shall have my daughters at my side through this difficult time. Both of them are so mature and successful. In their different ways. California! New York! I'm so proud. If only one of them had brought back a handsome boyfriend for me to seduce. —Wow. Did I just write that? Yes. Yes, in fact I did. Well, let it stand. —And what if he were tall and blond and bursting with pure masculine—

(The hideous sound of Bub's fiddle interrupts her. She slams her quill down)
Dammit!

SCENE FOURTEEN
The Judgment

It is late at night. Bub is practicing his fiddle. Karen, or some supernatural being that strongly resembles her, rides a tricycle into the room wearing a crown of thorns and a flowing white raiment. Bub stops what he's doing and observes her for a moment. Is he dreaming?

BUB: You gotta be kiddin' me. *Jesus?*

JESUS: Hi, Archie.

BUB: Oh, this is rich.

JESUS: I beg your pardon?

BUB: *My whole life* you pretend you don't exist, you ignore my cries of pain and despair, "I can't *hear* you, Archie, I don't *exist*, You're howling into the *void*..." And now, my last night on earth, when I *explicitly* asked you to stay the fuck away, what do you do? You come rolling in here on a goddamn *tricycle*—

JESUS: *(Overlapping)* Yeah, well, first of all, I never promised anything, and second of all, knock it off, Archie. I've got news for you.

BUB: Well, I don't want to hear it. Go away.

JESUS: You've been a very bad boy, Archie.

BUB: Who told you that, Jesus? Julia? The kids? Don't listen to them. They hate me. Plus, they're completely crazy! They'd have to be crazy to hate me. I'm a swell guy, Jesus. I mean, look: I built them a house with my own two hands!

JESUS: You call this a house?

BUB: At least I tried! It's the thought that counts, right? Didn't you say something like that in the, you know, the things, the…Gospels?

JESUS: Are you trying to throw me off track here, Archie?

BUB: No, no, Jesus. I'm just saying—

JESUS: *(Overlapping)* Because if you are, you might as well forget about it. One thing I do not do is get off track.

He dismounts from the tricycle. It's actually kind of scary.

BUB: Uh-oh.

JESUS: You got that right. So here's the thing, Archie: as soon as you've wrapped up your little "performance" here and you're just as dead as a really dead dead-guy, I'm going to send you somewhere…

BUB: Somewhere? You mean…?

JESUS: Yup…

Beat.

BUB: Aw, come on!

JESUS: I'm afraid so.

BUB: I haven't been *that* bad, have I?

JESUS: We've got high standards.

BUB: It's because I'm Jewish, isn't it?

JESUS: What? No.

BUB: Is it because I'm an atheist?

JESUS: That never really bothered me, actually.

BUB: Well, but, then, what did I do wrong, Jesus?

JESUS: I think you know.

Beat.

BUB: The fiddle...

JESUS: The fiddle.

BUB: *(Holding it aloft with a mixture of horror and fascination)* Sweet mother of Tommy Jarrell...

JESUS: Mood. So just let me summarize here. You are the direct descendent of His Excellency the Right Reverend Rabbi Ezekiel Finckelstein, Envoy to Emperor Charles V from the mythical Red Jews of Sambatyon. When you were a lad, your family vacationed at the most exclusive kibbutz in Tel Aviv. Your bar mitzvah was the talk of Brooklyn Heights in 1972. You graduated from Harvard at age 18 and Columbia Law at 20. You've read Proust cover to cover. Twice. In short, you are about as Jewish as a human being can possibly be. Which is all fine and good. I have nothing against that. Hell, I'm Jewish too, when it gets right down to it. Hence my question: what exactly do you think you're doing with that fiddle, Archie?

BUB: Lots of Jews play the fiddle, Jesus!

JESUS: In *Fiddler on the Roof* maybe. No, Archie, Jews play the *violin*.

BUB: But I *love* this music! You can't send me to Hell for loving something! That's not fair! It's not—Christian!

JESUS: Whoa, whoa, whoa. Back it up here.

BUB: What.

JESUS: You mentioned Hell just now.

BUB: Oh God!

JESUS: Calm down.

BUB: I'm going to Hell! It's probably even worse than Other People!

JESUS: Cut the crap, Archie.

BUB: I repent! I repent! I take it all back! I didn't mean any of it!

JESUS: Archie!

BUB: Hallelujah! Hallelujah!

JESUS: Archie! You will shut up now. Alright? Just put a sock in it. OK. Now, what's this? Are you being a wise guy with me? Is that what this is? You and I both know there's no such thing as Hell.

Beat.

BUB: There isn't?

JESUS: Duh. How long you been living among the goyim, Archie?

BUB: But, but, but—

JESUS: Of course there's no Hell! Didn't the Rabbi tell you that?

BUB: Well, he also told me the Messiah hadn't come yet, so as far as I'm concerned, all bets are off.

JESUS: You win some, you lose some. But take it from me: there is no Hell. Of course, there's no Heaven either, so there you go.

BUB: I knew it all along!

JESUS: Sure you did, Archie. Nope, all of it—reward and punishment—it all happens in this life. Or the next. Or the one after that. And so on.

BUB: Wait a minute: what?

JESUS: So here's the plan, Archie: as soon as you've pulled off your little *coup de théâtre* here tomorrow—which, let me assure you, I will make no attempt intervene in...

BUB: Thank you!

JESUS: ...I'm going to *reincarnate* you as...a West Virginia millworker! In the late 1880s! With...wait for it...*some actual musical talent!*

BUB: *(With dawning joy)* You're going to... Really?

JESUS: Sure, why not?

BUB: Oh my God! Jesus, this is fantastic news!

JESUS: Yeah, 'bout time you experienced what it's like to live a life that's nasty, brutish, and short. —Oh, and you won't mind being a syphilitic half-breed hermaphrodite with a harelip, will you?

Beat.

BUB: Um…

SCENE FIFTEEN
Musical Interludes Are So Depressing

Randall appears wearing a big red clown nose. He uses his Putt-Putt club from the earlier scene as a cane, and does a little singing soft-shoe routine. It's actually not that bad, in a schlumpy sort of way.

RANDALL: *(Singing)*
I'm just a schlumpy guy
I couldn't tell ya why
I don't expect you'll find me sympathetic

But I love my fiancée
She brightens up my day
Although she wishes I were more athletic

But at least I'm not a jerk
I show up on time to work
And if you ask I'll give you a donation

Or if I'm outta cash
I'll rummage in my stash
For just the thing to ease your alienation

But please don't get me wrong
I don't even own a bong
At least not since I graduated college

Uh-oh, I'm almost outta time
And still need one more rhyme
But now I'm drawing a blank except for "knowledge"

I know that's pretty lame
But hey, I didn't claim
To be the next Lord Tennyson or Snoop Dogg

Ah me, well such is life
But once Kristin is my wife
I'll never have to—

Whoops, I almost forgot
The engagement's kind of not
At least until the old man's six feet under

But after that we'll be
United in matrimony
Which let nobody ever put asund—

SCOTT: *(Emerging more or less out of nowhere)* Home slice! You spot me on the Putt-Putt? I totally left my wallet at the hotel.

RANDALL: Uh…sure.

SCOTT: You da man!

RANDALL: Don't mention it.

SCOTT: Yeah…yeah… And uh… Hey, can I ask you something?

RANDALL: What.

SCOTT: Do you ever look fat to yourself? I mean, when you're looking down at yourself?

RANDALL: Uh, I don't— What?

SCOTT: When you're looking down at yourself, like standing here, you know. Do you look fat to yourself?

RANDALL: *(Looking down at himself)* Uh…yeah. I guess.

SCOTT: Really?

RANDALL: Yeah. Sort of. Why?

SCOTT: Me too.

Beat.

RANDALL: Um…

SCOTT: Am I fat?

RANDALL: No.

SCOTT: Are you sure?

RANDALL: You look pretty fit to me, Scott.

SCOTT: Really?

RANDALL: Yeah.

SCOTT: Awesome. Thanks, man.

RANDALL: You're welcome.

Beat.

SCOTT: And you're right: I am fit! Hells to the yeah, I'm fit! Lean and mean, bro! Brought to you by DNA. Plus, I work out. And hey, since you're payin', why not let's hit the town? Like that new place down on the bypass, where I saw all the college ho's flaunting their juicy spank-pockets!

RANDALL: You mean…Skandalz?

SCOTT: Skandalz, bro! That's it! We're totally there. Giddyap, yo! The need for speed. Dude, I'm feelin' a tremendous masculine yang-surge in my quadriceps. Some lucky girl's gonna get more than her fair share tonight, oh yeah! Holiday bonus. BOGO. And then some. Damn! I'm getting excited. Where the fuck did I park?

SCENE SIXTEEN
The Three Sisters, Part 1

Kristin, Karen, and Kathryn sit on the stoop. Kristin sips from a mug of herbal tea, Karen from a bottle of cough syrup, Kathryn from a can of cheap beer.

KAREN: How can you drink that shit?

KATHRYN: It's easy. Watch. *(Chugs it, crushes the can, belches, gets another)*

KAREN: Jesus. You're too young to be able to do that.

KRISTIN: That is just so bad for you. Both of you. Alcohol like, totally inhibits your aura.

KAREN: Oh yeah?

KATHRYN: "Totally."

KRISTIN: *(Overlapping)* Totally. 'Cause like—shut up! 'Cause like, normally? It's like, out to here? Like, my aura for instance, right now? It reaches over to the recycling bin. At least. But your auras basically reach out to like, a little bit past your skin. Because of the alcohol.

KAREN: Speaking of, you notice how Mom's getting all splotchy?

KATHRYN: She's always been splotchy.

KAREN: No, but I mean actual red splotches.

KATHRYN: She's always had actual red splotches.

KAREN: Not like this.

KATHRYN: Dude. She's just too jacked up on Diet Coke to put her face on right anymore.

KAREN: At 6:00 a.m.? And don't call me "dude." Punk.

KRISTIN: It's the aspertene. That's what it does.

KATHRYN: I think you mean aspartame.

KRISTIN: Whatever, the stuff they put in there to make it sweet. It totally like, destroys your cells.

KATHRYN: Cool.

KAREN: Nothing can destroy Mom. Not even "aspertene."

They drink thoughtfully, each her beverage of choice.

KRISTIN: We did a yoga practice this morning.

KATHRYN: You and Mom?

KRISTIN: It was so great. We totally like, bonded.

KAREN: You got Mom in a yoga outfit?

KRISTIN: She loved it.

KAREN: No, seriously: Mom wore yoga tights?

KRISTIN: No, she wore some of Dad's old sweatpants. It was so awesome. I think it could be totally like, transformative for her. We did lots of like, twists and stuff. Yin yoga. It was very cleansing.

KATHRYN: Did she poop Dad's pants?

KAREN: *That's* what woke me up! There was this transcendental shit smell…

KRISTIN: Oh my God! You guys suck! You have no respect for yoga! I shouldn't even bother talking to you!

KAREN: Maybe you should get drunk with us. That would make it more fun.

KATHRYN: She is so beyond that.

KRISTIN: *(Overlapping)* I am so beyond—. Shut up! God!

KAREN: And I am so beyond horny right now.

KRISTIN: Gross!

KAREN: Yeah. It's weird. I'm never horny in the city. But I come back home and get a couple of drinks in me and I'm like ogling the high school boys at the Stop & Rob.

KATHRYN: You want me to make a few calls?

KAREN: Maybe. Is any of your friends like, *not* a greasy goth batshit freak-boy with raging acne?

KATHRYN: Um…no. But they all have huge dicks.

KRISTIN: Ew!

KAREN: Isn't there like, a home football game or something tonight?

KATHRYN: If there was, don't you think I'd be there with all my goth friends cheering for our team?

KAREN: Fuck you.

KRISTIN: Can we please talk about something like, serious? I mean, Dad is dying, guys!

Beat.

KAREN: Yup. There went my buzz.

KRISTIN: I mean, we did not come back home to like, get laid!

KAREN: Easy for you to say. You've got a lifelong sausage-fix lined up. And Katie's still looking for her clit.

KATHRYN: Actually I had it for a while there. But then I lost it again.

KRISTIN: Does Dad not even matter to you?

KAREN: You really think he's dying?

KRISTIN: Of course he's dying!

KATHRYN: We're all dying.

KRISTIN: He's got a terrible disease!

KAREN: Give him a break. He's married to Mom. Isn't that bad enough?

KATHRYN: Maybe that's the disease she's talking about.

KRISTIN: No, he's got—! I saw the—thing, the—whatever they call it! The picture-gram!

KAREN: So you really think Dad's dying.

KRISTIN: Yes!

KAREN: It's not just another one of his publicity stunts.

KRISTIN: You don't really love him, do you?

KAREN: Do you?

KRISTIN: Of course!

KAREN: Katie?

KATHRYN: What.

KAREN: Do you love Dad?

KATHRYN: Sort of. Yeah. I guess. I mean, I don't actually know him all that well.

SCENE SEVENTEEN
The Big Mistake

Scott and Randall sit at the bar in "Skandalz," the scuzziest of all scuzzy undergraduate meat-market scuzz-buckets. They have to shout a bit over the music.

SCOTT: No shit, bro? You're gettin' hitched?

RANDALL: Yeah. I mean, we haven't set a—

SCOTT: The little goth punk? You sure she won't murder you in your sleep?

RANDALL: No, not her. Ha, ha. No. It's her older sister.

SCOTT: Well, damn, son! I gotta see this. Who's the sad little wench? Lemme guess: geometry teacher.

RANDALL: No.

SCOTT: Librarian?

RANDALL: No.

SCOTT: Substitute bus driver?

RANDALL: No, she's not connected with the school.

SCOTT: Aw shit. Don't tell me it's some old maid plays the bass fiddle in that hillbilly music thing.

RANDALL: Actually she's a yoga teacher.

Beat.

SCOTT: Fuck me.

RANDALL: Well, I mean she's studying to be a yoga teacher. One day she'll be a yoga teacher.

SCOTT: Dude, that is so hot! This one chick? Fort Lauderdale, working on a job down there, back when I was doing asphalt with Blankenship, right? Parking lot for a new Walmart. Anyway, this chick. Yoga teacher, right? Met her at the gym. The sweetest little squeeze-box you'd ever wanna, and she could like, bend it all around and shit? I never knew where it was gonna end up next. It was like spearing catfish, I swear. She wanted me to do yoga with her, right? Practice or whatever, but we always ended up in some *Kama Sutra* thing with her ass in my face and my dick flying around somewhere. It was crazy.

Beat.

RANDALL: Um…

SCOTT: So do I know her?

RANDALL: Who?

SCOTT: The bee-trothed, bro!

RANDALL: I doubt it. I mean, she's from here, but she's younger than us.

SCOTT: Dude, so who is it?

RANDALL: You probably know her folks, though. The Finckelsteins.

SCOTT: Finckelstein? Huh…

RANDALL: Yeah, they, uh, well anyway, and there are three sisters. You met Katie, the youngest. Kristin is the eldest. That's my, uh, girlfriend.

SCOTT: What about the middle one? Is she a yoga teacher too?

RANDALL: No.

SCOTT: Too bad. So you got a picture?

RANDALL: Of Kristin? Uh…not really. I mean, I have a picture from when she was in high school. She was a cheerleader…

He fishes an ancient picture carefully out of his wallet, shows it. Beat.

SCOTT: That's her?

RANDALL: Yeah.

SCOTT: Whoa…

RANDALL: I know. She's really very beautiful.

SCOTT: Where did you find that?

RANDALL: I cut it out of her yearbook.

SCOTT: No, I mean *that,* dude, *her.* Where did you meet her?

RANDALL: At your wedding, actually.

SCOTT: You're shittin' me. And where was I?

RANDALL: Uh…getting married?

They look at the picture a moment longer. Then Randall puts it away.

SCOTT: Hey! Let's go over there! You can totally introduce me!

RANDALL: Um…

SCOTT: *(Getting up)* Come on, bro! Let's roll.

RANDALL: Well, it's kinda late…

SCOTT: The night is young!

RANDALL: Yeah, but Mr. Finckelstein isn't doing well these days.

SCOTT: All the better, bro! We can take the girls out, give the old man some peace and quiet.

RANDALL: No, Scott. Seriously. I don't think it's a good idea.

SCOTT: It's a rockin' idea! What's wrong with you, homes? You used to be down for a good time. Now, it's like you're all schlumped-out and lame.

RANDALL: I'm just—. I don't think—.

SCOTT: Look. We get there, it's sleepy time, we split. Plus, I got an early start tomorrow on this new job anyway, so it's not gonna be like, *all night*. I just wanna meet these people my best man's planning on spending the rest of his life with. Make sure they're up to snuff. You gotta give me that, bro.

RANDALL: OK. OK. Fine. But I really think we should call first and make sure—

SCOTT: *(Overlapping, already on his way out)* Done. Oh, and uh, be sure to leave a good tip. The waitress gave me a sweet blow out back.

SCENE EIGHTEEN
The Three Sisters, Part 2

As before.

KAREN: *(Starting to get up)* Well, look, bitches. It's been great, but I can't handle this anymore. I need to go masturbate like, right now, so you guys just talk amongst yourselves.

KRISTIN: *(To Kathryn)* And Mom said you told Karen he's plotting something. Why would you even like, say that?

KAREN: *(Dizzy, sitting back down)* Whoa there…better take it slow…

KATHRYN: I didn't say "plotting." I said "planning."

KRISTIN: "Planning," whatever. How do you know?

KATHRYN: He's just been super sneaky lately. Staying down in the man cave all the time. I went down there last week and as soon as he saw me, he shoved these papers in his desk and locked it.

KRISTIN: What papers?

KATHRYN: How should I know?

KAREN: Probably the *Hillbilly Manifesto*. He's been working on it for twenty years.

KRISTIN: Maybe it's his Last Will and Testicles.

Beat.

KAREN: Um, did you just say—?

KATHRYN: *(Overlapping)* Hey look. A monster truck just pulled into the drive.

KRISTIN: Oh my God. That is so redneck.

KATHRYN: Maybe it's the high school quarterback slash coke dealer.

KAREN: My prayers are answered!

KRISTIN: Wait a minute. I know that guy. Isn't that…uh…?

KATHRYN: Randall? Your fiancé?

KRISTIN: Who? Oh. Right. Ex-fiancé.

KATHRYN: What?

KAREN: The Schlumpster? What's he doing driving Biff's monster truck? —Uh oh: and that gorgeous hunk of man-meat must be Biff…

KATHRYN: Oh shit…

KAREN: Scratch the masturbation plan. —Over here, boys! Over here! Yeah! Hooweee! —Oh my God, he is so beautiful. Let's just hope he's not gay. Hey, is the hot tub on?

SCENE NINETEEN
Bromance

Randall's basement apartment. Scott and Randall wear swimming trunks. Randall still wears a T-shirt. Scott admires himself in the mirror.

SCOTT: Thanks, bro. A little dorky, but hey. The pecs make up for it, right?

RANDALL: Definitely.

SCOTT: *(Doing Eddie Murphy doing James Brown)* "It's hot in the hot tub! Jump back! Kiss myself! Huh!"

RANDALL: I hate hot tubs.

SCOTT: Why?

RANDALL: They make me feel sleazy.

SCOTT: That's the point! And I *still cannot believe* you've been sitting on this treasure trove of top-grade babe-idge all these years! They're both so hot! But I gotta say: the back lot on your fiancée? That is some prime real estate, bro. Bravo.

RANDALL: Um, yeah, I need to clarify something, Scott.

SCOTT: Hey man, I've been waiting for clarification all night.

He begins preparing a line of coke. Randall is somewhat taken aback.

RANDALL: Yeah, uh, so about Kristin and me. The thing is that, well, technically, we're not actually, uh… Hey, do you really think you should be doing that here?

SCOTT: What.

RANDALL: The, uh…

SCOTT: It's just a little pick-me-up, homes! I gotta be in top form for what's about to happen in the happenin' hot tub, yo!

RANDALL: What's about to happen in the happenin' hot tub?

SCOTT: Dude. Did you see the way the middle one was drooling over the McPackage? And did you see her in that microscopic *bikini,* bro? Need I say more?

RANDALL: Well, but I don't think now is the time to—

SCOTT: Plus, dude. You got your own little junction box all juiced up and ready to go. "Fee-an-say!" *(Snorts a massive line)* Whooo! *Yeah!* That's what I'm talkin' 'bout! *(Throws a few punches)*

RANDALL: Actually, that's the thing. If you could maybe not refer to her as my fiancée in front of her?

   Beat.

SCOTT: The fuck?

RANDALL: It's just, she's kind of sensitive about it right now. Her Dad being sick and all. It's kind of, um, a rough time she's going through, and we've decided, I mean, mutually, considering the various stresses and all, that it's best if we—

SCOTT: *(Overlapping)* She broke up with you.

RANDALL: No! No. No. I mean, not really. Not permanently. It's just sort of, um, a temporary, um, hiatus, so that she can focus on—

SCOTT: *(Overlapping)* Holy shit, bro. You know what this means?

RANDALL: Um, no. What?

SCOTT: *(A beatific vision)* It means…I get…both of them…!

RANDALL: What?

SCOTT: I get both of them!

He grabs Randall, starts humping him.

RANDALL: Jesus! Put me down!

Thrasher music.

SCOTT: *(Singing)*
A girly on the left
A girly on the right
And me in the middle
All damn night

I get both of them! Yeah, yeah!
I get both of them! Yeah, yeah!

I slap 'em up one side
I slap 'em down the other
I flip 'em like a pancake
And cover 'em with butter

I get both of them! Yeah, yeah!
I get both of them! Yeah, yeah!

Gimme gimme gimme gimme
Gimme gimme ha!

Gimme gimme gimme gimme
Gimme gi—
   (The music stops on a dime. He drops Randall)
Hey, what's the mom look like?

Act Three

SCENE TWENTY
Beyond the River Sambatyon

It's early morning. Bub sits in his wheelchair by the window, air rifle at the ready. He sees something out the window, slowly raises the rifle, aims it.

BUB: That's right, you little bastard. Come on... Come on around the mountain... *(Shoots and misses)* Dammit!

KATHRYN: *(Entering)* Dad? It's five in the morning.

BUB: *(Re: the rifle)* This piece of shit. What I need is a shotgun. Something with some goddamn *spread*. Take out three of those fuckers at once. Little puffs of fur. Piff, piff, piff.

KATHRYN: Yeah, but you'd probably take out the bird feeder too.

BUB: It would be worth it. God, I hate squirrels. You'd think on my last day on earth I'd get to murder at least one of those little sonsabitches. *(Sighs with a vague longing)*

KATHRYN: Well, happy birthday.

BUB: Thanks. Who are you?

KATHRYN: I'm your daughter. Kathryn.

BUB: Really? What do you want?

KATHRYN: Well, you're dying and stuff, so I thought maybe we should get to know each other before you go.

BUB: Why?

KATHRYN: Good question.

BUB: Oh, I'm full of good questions. You have no idea.

KATHRYN: I guess it's mostly for my benefit. You know, a little last-ditch effort to break through the wall, so I don't grow up thinking all men are aloof and full of spite.

BUB: But I am aloof and full of spite.

KATHRYN: Damn.

BUB: But don't worry, kid: that's probably just me.

KATHRYN: What are you spiteful about?

BUB: Aw, shucks, I don't know. Maybe the fact that I'm *dying* and nobody *feeds* me!

KATHRYN: Are you hungry?

BUB: No. And even if I were, I'd refuse to eat.

KATHRYN: Why?

BUB: Because I'm full of spite!

KATHRYN: Makes sense. Well, nice to meet you anyway.

BUB: Ditto. Say, you mind handing me that box of pellets?
(She hands him the box of pellets and pulls up a chair beside him. Through the following, he breaks down the rifle, reloads, prepares to shoot at another squirrel)
So. You're my daughter. Funny, I always had the feeling there was someone else around here. I mean, besides the schlump in the basement. I gotta say, though, kid, you've kept a pretty low profile.

KATHRYN: Seemed like the thing to do.

BUB: What, the hysterical feminine wombat looniness around here doesn't appeal to you?

KATHRYN: Meh...

BUB: Which reminds me. What was all that yelling about last night? Sounded like a damn frat party in the basement.

KATHRYN: It was a frat party in the basement.

BUB: Shouldn't you and your sisters at least wait until I'm actually dead?

KATHRYN: Hey, don't ask me. I stayed in my room.

BUB: Really?

KATHRYN: Really.

BUB: My imminent death doesn't make you want to party like it's 1999?

KATHRYN: I mean, I watched for a while, but then it got stupid.

BUB: Huh. Well, I wish I'd known all this a lot sooner. I could have enlisted you in the fight. Sort of a counter-insurgency ninja-type double-agent thing. I like that.

KATHRYN: I'm all about me some ninjas.

BUB: Too late now. I'll be dead in a matter of hours here, one way or another. And after that I'll be safely ensconced in the 1880s, so who gives a shit. *(Takes aim at a squirrel)*

KATHRYN: I do have one question, though.

BUB: Go for it.

KATHRYN: Did you really never love us, like Mom says?

He shoots. Sound of breaking glass.

BUB: Goddammit!

KATHRYN: Time for a new bird feeder, eh?

Beat.

BUB: Look kid: —What's your name again?

KATHRYN: Kathryn.

BUB: Look, Kathryn: you seem like a nice kid, now that we've gotten to know each other a little.

KATHRYN: Thanks.

BUB: Though the vampire makeup kinda freaks me out.

KATHRYN: Good.

BUB: What's up with that?

KATHRYN: I'm performing a compensatory psychological function by symbolically manifesting the repressed contents.

BUB: What contents?

KATHRYN: All the dark shit we don't talk about.

BUB: Oh. That. Right. What was I saying?

KATHRYN: I don't know. You hadn't said it yet.

BUB: Huh. Maybe I was finished.

KATHRYN: Maybe.

BUB: Well, anyway. Now that I'm considering the bird feeder I've just inadvertently shot to pieces, it occurs to me that I haven't paid you a lot of attention in life. I'm sorry about that. But look at it this way: it's made you strong and self-reliant.

KATHRYN: Has it?

BUB: Hasn't it?

KATHRYN: I think it's made me kind of bitter and cynical.

BUB: Could be. But at least you're not selfish, like your mother and sisters. And besides, it was the best I could do. Think about it! I've been married to your mother for forty years! *That's forty years I can never have back!* It's a miracle I can even speak. It's a miracle I haven't tied you all to the bird feeder and let the squirrels eat your eyeballs out while I sit here by the window laughing maniacally.

KATHRYN: Yeah, I guess now that you put it that way, I've got a lot to be thankful for.

BUB: Yes, you do. I was a happy Jew Boy once. Well, not happy exactly, but studious and mostly content. Brooklyn was a good place to grow up back in those days. I felt safe. I did well in school. My family had high hopes for me. I was going to take over my Uncle Gershom's law practice. But I made a crucial mistake.

KATHRYN: What was that?

BUB: I took a night off.

KATHRYN: Oh.

BUB: Yeah, one of my law school buddies, this rich WASP from Memphis, persuaded me to go with him to a party in the East Village.

KATHRYN: Sounds fun.

BUB: It was. Until I woke up naked in the bathtub with a shaved wingding and a splitting headache. And somehow I knew.

KATHRYN: Knew what?

BUB: I'd been deflowered.

KATHRYN: You mean, you were…date-raped?

BUB: Come to find out, that quote unquote friend of mine was basically a pimp for penniless debutantes of dubious character, a.k.a. your mother. In fact, it was all an elaborate setup to get her hitched to an upwardly mobile young Jew from a good family.

KATHRYN: Are you serious?

BUB: Oh, it was a big thing back in those days, unbeknownst to me. Why, they had a whole underground railroad going: Memphis to Manhattan. Last Stop: Finckelstein.

KATHRYN: That sucks.

BUB: Tell me about it.

KATHRYN: But still. Couldn't you just have, I don't know, *dealt* with it and gone on with your life?

BUB: *Dealt* with it? *Dealt* with it?! How? You think they would let me take over Uncle Gershom's law practice after having mingled with a moth-eaten shiksa? Much less married one! I was ruined! I had brought shame and disgrace upon my entire family! The line was broken! They handed me a check and said "Scram!" So I did. I scrammed.

KATHRYN: Jeeze, Dad. I'm sorry to hear all that.

BUB: It's your own fault. You asked.

KATHRYN: True.

Beat.

BUB: Well, I'm glad we've had this conversation, kid. You're easy to talk to. I feel a little better now. Lighter somehow. A shared sorrow and all that. Thanks.

KATHRYN: You're welcome. But you still haven't answered my question.

BUB: What question?

KATHRYN: Mom says you never really loved us. Is that true?

Beat.

BUB: Your mother and I got off on the wrong foot. You can understand that, can't you? I married her out of guilt. She married me out of desperation. That's no way to start anything.

KATHRYN: I guess not.

BUB: But look. Kathryn. This was all years ago. Before you were even a twinkle of hate-lust in your mother's eye. So it's not your fault, OK? You don't have to "compensate" or whatever. Getting married was a huge mistake, but it was *our* mistake. If we'd been better people, we would have been able to make the best of it. But we weren't better people. We were exactly who we were, warts and all. We disappointed each other from day one. We couldn't let go of our expectations. And they weren't even *our* expectations! They were somebody else's! My father's! Her mother's! I mean, how stupid is that?

KATHRYN: Pretty stupid, actually.

BUB: Catastrophically stupid! And here we are!

KATHRYN: Yeah.

BUB: But don't worry, kid. You'll do better, trust me. You'll find love someday. Just make sure it's completely different from everything you've had occasion to observe here.

KATHRYN: But what if it's someone I can't have?

BUB: Perfect. You'll never be disappointed.

KATHRYN: Right.

BUB: Now: all this sentimentality has loosened my bowels, and I have to poop like a gorilla. So how about you go get what's-his-face, your sister's fiancé in here to, uh, lend me a hand.

KATHRYN: Will do. *(Turns to go)*

BUB: And one more thing, before I forget.

KATHRYN: What.

BUB: I'm not actually your father.

Beat.

KATHRYN: Um…what?

BUB: Yeah. I wasn't going to tell you just yet, but the fact is you and your siblings were spawned from the unholy union of your depraved mother and a rancid incubus named Baalzebluglug.

KATHRYN: Baalzebluglug.

BUB: And a couple of his buddies whose names I can never remember.

KATHRYN: Um…OK.

BUB: Dark family secret: we're not actually a family. Well: you guys are. Sort of.

KATHRYN: You know, that actually explains a lot.

BUB: I know, right? —Oh look! The sun's coming up! Sunrise on the morning of my last day among the living! Kinda nice the way it glitters in the broken glass of the bird feeder, eh? Ah, me. Maybe I shoulda been a poet after all…

Music starts up: a sort of country-western crooner song. Kathryn exits.

BUB: *(Singing)*
Beyond the River Sambatyon
There dwell the Ten Lost Tribes

A mighty host of Jewishness!
Impervious to bribes!

The river rages day and night
And none can dare to cross
But on the holy Sabbath day
The waters lie like dross.

But dammit, it's the Sabbath!
The Jews are barred from travel!
So there they sit upon the shore
While gulls poke at the gravel.

But ah! The day shall soon arrive
When Yahweh lifts his hand
And sends Messiah down to earth
To smite all Edom's land—oy!—

And then the Jews of Sambatyon
Shall surge across the ford
And kick some serious goyim ass
In the true name of the Lord!

SCENE TWENTY-ONE
The Big-Ass Party

Everyone in the family is now seated around a table. Well, everyone except for Kristin, who's sitting rather fiercely in lotus position on her yoga mat on the floor; Kathryn, who's curled up under the table reading a Russian novel with her earphones on; and Karen, who appears to be so hungover she can't hold her head up off the table. Julia looks better than she has in years and is thinking about why. Only Randall appears to be in any way attentive, although he looks utterly derelict.

BUB: Is this everybody?

JULIA: Why shouldn't it be?

BUB: I feel like someone's missing. Your demon lover maybe?

JULIA: He always comes later.

BUB: Frankly, I don't see how he manages to *come* at all.

JULIA: Not everyone is afflicted with your *shortcomings,* dear.

KAREN: "And they're off!"

RANDALL: I think we're all here, sir.

BUB: How nice of everybody to be here for my birthday! Especially since it's going to be my last one. Nothing like an impending death to bring American families together! Why, looky here: my daughter Kristin has arrived all the way from…wherever she was, doing…whatever she was doing. And my other—

KRISTIN: San Francisco, Dad. Studying yoga!

BUB: Right. Yoga. How fascinating and useful. And my other daughter, Karen, is here all the way from that septic tank of iniquity known as New York, where she is doubtless debauching herself on a nightly basis.

KAREN: Guilty as charged.

BUB: Which is all very moving. But here let me register my pleasant surprise at discovering, this very morning, as I was attempting to assassinate a squirrel, that I have yet a third daughter, allegedly named Kathryn, who is not quite as idiotic as the rest of you. A small blessing, and a belated one, I confess, but one I shall not disdain to count on this my very last birthday on earth.

JULIA: Nonsense! You'll outlive me just to make sure I never get a new kitchen.

BUB: I admit that would be a pleasure worth hanging on for. Nevertheless, the time has come—

JULIA: *(Overlapping)* Well, I'm planning on living to be a hundred and five, buster, so you'd better just buckle the fuck on down!

KRISTIN: Mom!

JULIA: I'm just feeling so great today!

KRISTIN: OK, but maybe you could like, not express it in a negative manner? It's Dad's last birthday!

JULIA: I know. Isn't that wonderful?

KRISTIN: How can you say that?

BUB: Don't try to reason with it. I've been trying for four decades. It's hopeless. You might as well talk ethics to a rabid rottweiler.

JULIA: Now you kids see what I've been suffering in secret. Every day!

KAREN: The open hostility is kind of a relief, actually.

BUB: Hostility doesn't begin to describe the moral atrocities to which your mother has subjected me from the very first day of our ill-fated—

KRISTIN: Mom! Dad! Everybody! Please, let's just take a big deep breath together and let all the negativity melt away like, like clouds on a warm slice of birthday cake!

Beat.

BUB: That doesn't make any sense.

RANDALL: Kristin's right, sir. We're here to celebrate your birthday, and to wish you many happy returns.

BUB: You. Wait a minute…banjo player…

RANDALL: Randall, sir. We had a long talk yesterday about—

BUB: *(Overlapping)* Randall! Ah! Now I remember! The pseudo-hillbilly who wants to marry the pseudo-yoga teacher!

RANDALL: That's right, sir. I mean, that's not exactly, uh—

KRISTIN: We're not getting married.

RANDALL: Kristin, I think—

JULIA: Oh, thank God!

KRISTIN: I wasn't going to tell you, Dad, 'cause I didn't want to upset you, 'cause I know you like, um, appreciate Randy, even though he lives in the basement, and also you're proud of me for finally settling down and stuff.

BUB: I am?

KRISTIN: But I just really wanted to totally be here for you in this difficult time of transition and stuff, and being engaged to Randy would really distract me from that.

RANDALL: And I just want to say that I support Kristin completely in whatever she feels is the right thing to do for herself. I mean, for you. For everybody. Because I love her. You.

Karen has started snoring.

BUB: *(Genuinely surprised)* You actually are a semi-decent guy.

RANDALL: I hope so, sir.

BUB: Remember that in a minute here. I'm gonna need you running your A game.

RANDALL: Sir?

BUB: Just a little heads-up. And while I'm thinking of it, who the fuck is that?

They turn to look. Yes, it's Scott, freshly showered, wrapped in a towel, convincingly resembling the stud he is.

SCOTT: Awesome water pressure up here, dude.

JULIA: There you are! We've been waiting!

KAREN: *(Waking up)* What…? Oh, God…

SCOTT: Well, you know how it is—there's just so much of me to get lathered up! Takes a while.

BUB: Would someone mind explaining to me—?

JULIA: *(Overlapping)* Come sit with mama…

SCOTT: Oh, now, you know what's gonna happen if I sit next to you, baby… *(Sits beside her; very snuggly.)*

BUB: The hell?

KRISTIN: Dad, this is Brad. Brad Superfine. He's my guru.

JULIA: Nonsense! His name is Dave Blankenship. My first love! And he's all mine. Right, girls?

KAREN: His name is Biff Chomsky, the high school quarterback, and he was supposed to be mine!

KRISTIN: Mine!

KAREN: He wanted me first!

KRISTIN: He wanted you *at* first!

SCOTT: Girls! We had the contest. And Julia here won fair and square.

JULIA: Ha!

Beat.

RANDALL: Actually his name is Scott.

BUB: Scott, Brad, Biff, Dave, Doug, Danny the Dalai Lama. Bullshit. I know who this is. This is—this can only be: Baalzebluglug!

SCOTT: *(Laughs)* That's good. Mr. Finckelstein, great to meet you.

BUB: Charmed. And what, pray tell, are you doing at my birthday party?

KRISTIN: Dad! He's in town visiting, and we thought the more the merrier, you know? Share the love and stuff.

RANDALL: Share the love, sir. Yes.

BUB: You witches summoned this two-bit incubus to my birthday party?

JULIA: But really I summoned him. Didn't I, Dave?

SCOTT: Well, but hey! If Mr. Finckelstein isn't down with it…

KRISTIN: No, Brad! You can stay!

KAREN: We all want you to stay, Biff.

KRISTIN: He can stay, can't he, Dad?

JULIA: He can stay.

BUB: What? No! No, no, no! This is all wrong! It's *my* birthday party! It's *my Gesamtkunstwerk*! It's *my* last chance to bring you all down in a fiery implosion of screams and twisted metal! This is a private affair!

JULIA: What are you raving about this time? I baked the cake!

BUB: Schlumpy, back me up on this!

RANDALL: Well, I guess it is a little bit presumptuous to invite someone who—

JULIA: Shut up, Schlumpy. Now. Everybody. Listen up and listen up good. I baked the friggin' cake, and I want Dave here. Come to think of it, I want him everywhere else too. Got it?

KAREN: But seriously. Isn't she a little old for you, Biff?

KRISTIN: Um, yeah!

JULIA: Tell them what you told me last night, Dave. I've been saving it up, haven't I?

KAREN: I'm not even gonna tell you what Biff told me. It's too nasty.

KRISTIN: What Brad told me was like, so beautiful and true… all my chakras were just drinking it in…like an awesome goji berry CBD smoothie…with sprinkles on top!

BUB: So let me get this straight. All three of you humped the demon?

JULIA: In no particular order…

KAREN, KRISTIN, AND JULIA: And then all at once.

SCOTT: That rocked.

BUB: Sodom and Gomorrah under my very own roof. Somehow I knew it would come to this. I was just hoping to be dead before it happened.

RANDALL: Sir, I tried to stop them, but they wouldn't listen to me.

BUB: Welcome to my world, kid.

SCOTT: Well anyway, I gotta roll, yo.

JULIA: What? No!

SCOTT: Yep. Big job today. The boys are probably wondering where the boss man is.

JULIA: Aren't you going to stay for cake?

SCOTT: Baby, you know I'd love to, but I'm late as it is. How about you save me a big piece?

JULIA: You can have all of it. Every day. Over and over again. *(Hands him the cake)*

SCOTT: Cool. Well, *adiós, muchachos y muchachas!* It's been real! *(Exits with the cake)*

JULIA: *(Calling after him)* Au revoir, mon amour!

BUB: Disgusting.

JULIA: The world is full of joy and love.

KAREN: You gave the cake away, Mom. Nice move.

JULIA: Shall I bake a new one? Or maybe just dig around in the fridge for some prehistoric banana bread?

BUB: *(Glancing at his watch)* Leave it. The moment has arrived. *(Rises from his wheelchair without any particular effort)* Bitches, hos and harpies, lend me your ears. I've got a goddamn announcement to make.

JULIA: *(Eagerly)* You'll be dead before we get to the melted ice cream?

BUB: Yes. But that's not all. I also happen to have on my person a certain document. A letter, actually. *(Removes letter from pocket, unfolds it)* Dated…let's see…ah! One year ago today! What a coincidence. From…the Vice President of New Resources Development at Blastmax Energies, Inc.

RANDALL: Blastmax Energies?

BUB: Namely, a certain Robert Whitten Linklater III, who wishes to convey to me his interest in purchasing the mineral rights to this my modest tract of land for purposes of…you guessed it: fracking. *(Holds up the letter)*

RANDALL: Good God, sir!

JULIA: What's fracking?

KAREN: I'll tell you later, Mom.

BUB: Moreover, for the purchase of aforementioned rights, Mr. Linklater humbly offers me the tight little sum of… One Hundred and Twenty-Three Million Dollars. And some change. *(Calmly folds up the letter, returns it to his pocket)*

JULIA: Oh my God...!

KAREN: Damn!

KRISTIN: Awesome!

BUB: I know, I know. You're all thinking: "We're rich! We're rich! As soon as the old Jew dies, we'll inherit the land, sell it off, and live like Pharaoh's Concubines to the end of our days!"

RANDALL: I wasn't thinking that, sir.

KRISTIN: I'll start my own yoga studio and retreat center in Costa Rica!

KAREN: Fuck Law School! I'm moving straight to Central Park West!

JULIA: A new kitchen! With Dave! In his boxer briefs!

BUB: Doesn't that all just sound fantastic? Well, dream on, bitches. 'Cause here's the hitch: you're not getting one red cent. Why? Because...drum roll please... *We're Not Actually a Family!*
  (Dead silence)
Aren't you supposed to at least gasp in horror or something?

JULIA: *(Horrified)* Archibald!

BUB: That's more like it.

JULIA: Archibald! You promised me you'd never—! He's raving! It's the drugs!

BUB: Well, I'm breaking my promise, Julia. Kids: you're not my kids. I'll let your mother explain that one. Or maybe "Dave/Scott/Brad/Biff" would care to. Anyway, I'm happy to report that you're no spawn of mine. And as for your dubious mother, she and I never actually got married, thanks to her Jew-hating father, who threatened to hang my testicles from his gun rack. Which, in retrospect, was the nicest thing the white trash sonuvabitch ever did for me. Now—

JULIA: Lies! Lies and mendacity! Don't listen to him, kids! You are the fruit of this man's rancid loins, and he never loved you! He never loved any of us! He's a monster!

BUB: Yes, well, that's been the story for a long time, hasn't it? He never loved us, we're the victims, boo-hoo, boo-hoo. But the truth of the matter is—

RANDALL: *(Overlapping)* Um, sir? Sir!

BUB: What, Schlumpy? I'm kind of in the middle of my speech here.

RANDALL: I know. I hate to interrupt, but what is that noise?

Yes: a distant, subterranean rumbling/cracking noise is heard.

BUB: Oh. Well. Yes. How quickly things move! I'm impressed.

RANDALL: But what is it? It's not… I mean, it can't be—

BUB: *(Overlapping)* That, praise Jesus, is the sound of modern natural gas extraction technology. It is also the sound of this house and everything in it about to be sucked down into the sulfurous pit of eternity!

RANDALL: *(Standing up)* Oh my God!

KRISTIN: What?

KAREN: Uh-oh.

JULIA: What's going on? I don't understand any of this! What's happening?

The sound is growing louder.

BUB: *(Laughing maniacally)* Yes, bitches! Welcome to the Apocalypse!

The sound is deafening. Everyone is frozen in terror.
There's an explosion somewhere under the house. Bub raises his arms in victory, fiddle and bow in hand. Everyone screams.
Randall snaps out of it. Like a superhero—with appropriate musical accompaniment—he carries the women one by one to safety: Kristin, Karen, and Julia. He then reaches to help Bub, who furiously holds him at bay by swinging his fiddle like a club. He then realizes Kathryn has been oblivious to it all, thanks to her headphones. He reaches under the table, pulls her free, carries her to safety, then goes back one last time for Bub, who once again forces him away. At the last moment, Randall turns and escapes. Bub is left alone, sawing madly at his fiddle as the house collapses around him. His fiddling swells into a massive orchestral "Dies Irae." A tremendous crash as the entire house and surrounding outbuildings are sucked down into the frack-void.
Fade to BLACKOUT over sounds of splintering wood, ruptured plumbing, distressed chickens, bewildered cows, frantic squirrels, popping fiddle strings, bookshelves spilling their stacks of Foxfire *back issues—all tumbling into oblivion.*
A thoughtful pause.
Then the plaintive pop of one last fiddle string.
Then a lonely chicken.

Lights up on a pasture near the crater. All stare in disbelief at what has happened.

JULIA: It's over.

KRISTIN: He's gone.

KAREN: It's all gone.

KATHRYN: Wow.
(They all look at her)
What.

They look back at the crater.

JULIA: Oh my God… I'm free… I'm finally free!

KRISTIN: You've always been free, Mom. That's the neat thing about yoga, is you like, totally embrace your inner freedom and joy and stuff that was always there and like, give yourself permission to be happy for ever and ever.

JULIA: No. I mean, I'm actually free. The curse is broken.

KAREN: What is she talking about?

JULIA: A whole new life! A second chance! In Florida! Never, ever, ever to return to this clay-sucking cultural backwater devoid of sunshine! Dave?… Where are you, my love…? *(Departs in giddy anticipation)*

KAREN: I give it a week before he ditches her at SeaWorld.

KRISTIN: You always resented other people's bliss…

KAREN: That's true. Especially when it was supposed to be my bliss. Well, anyway… Guys, it was fun. Really. But now I'm heading back to New York to be privileged and complain about it. —I know, I know, "embrace the ice cream of joy" and all that shit, but the truth is, I actually like being pissed off and miserable. Strange, I know, but hey. Genetics. Which reminds me: since we're at best really only half-sisters, I'd prefer not to think of us as related at all. Sort of the glass half-empty kinda thing, you know? Nothing personal. So: have a nice life, and fuck off. *(Exits)*

KRISTIN: That was so mean.

KATHRYN: What did you expect?

Beat.

KRISTIN: Well, I guess it's my turn.

RANDALL: Honey—er, sweetheart, Kristin, before you say anything, I just want you to know I understand how you're probably feeling pretty confused right now, I mean with all that's happened, but I still love you and I'll wait for you for however long you—

KRISTIN: *(Overlapping)* Wait, what? No. Confused? Believe me, I'm totally like, not confused.

RANDALL: Oh. You're not? Does this mean…?

KRISTIN: Yesterday? After we broke up and it was my turn to have sex with Brad in the hot tub? I totally had this like, awesome epiphany.

RANDALL: Um…that's really…

KRISTIN: All these attachments, you know? I don't need them. I'm like, so much happier on my own. I need to be free! Free to do what I want to do! Free to go to California, and Costa Rica, and Bali, and India! For as long as I want! Free to take awesome selfies using my selfie stick. Free to have intimate epiphanies with other totally free people, people who don't expect anything from me! All my life I've been surrounded by these totally like, needy people who need me for my light and my joyfulness and my beautiful spontaneous feminine essence, and I just don't need that anymore. I need to be free from all that neediness.

RANDALL: Oh.

KRISTIN: That's what I need.

RANDALL: Well, but maybe if I—

KRISTIN: *(Overlapping)* It feels so good to have made my decision. I'm leaving now. I really am. Goodbye…uh…

KATHRYN: Randall.

KRISTIN: Goodbye, Randall! Goodbye forever! Thanks for loving me the best way you knew how!

RANDALL: Um…OK…

KRISTIN: And thanks for being so nice to my Dad.

RANDALL: You're welcome.

KRISTIN: Oh! And for saving everybody just now. That was like, super sweet of you.

RANDALL: I try.

KRISTIN: And bye, little Katie! I don't like you!

KATHRYN: Ditto! Bye!

Wearing a beatific smile, Kristin does a brief yoga posture, then floats away forever. Beat.

RANDALL: Do you think she meant that?

KATHRYN: What.

RANDALL: All that stuff about goodbye forever.

KATHRYN: Um…*yeah.*

RANDALL: Dammit!

KATHRYN: Really?

RANDALL: I thought we were going to be together for the rest of our lives!

KATHRYN: You were never together in the first place.

RANDALL: Don't be a jerk. I put everything into that relationship. Everything! My love! My hopes and dreams! A couple grand for yoga teacher training!

KATHRYN: Dude. You can't be in a relationship by yourself.

RANDALL: You don't understand! It's—. No, no, no, that's— that's—. Huh.

KATHRYN: You're over thirty and you don't know that?

RANDALL: I guess I was sort of hoping…

KATHRYN: Kidding yourself is what you were doing.

RANDALL: Ouch.

Beat.

KATHRYN: Well. Goodbye, I guess.

RANDALL: Yeah. Goodbye.

They look at each other for a moment.

KATHRYN: I always thought you were cool.

RANDALL: Really?

KATHRYN: Yeah. Really. I even wrote a song about you.

RANDALL: Thanks. I guess.

KATHRYN: You're welcome.

Beat.

RANDALL: Actually, can we stay here a little longer? I just feel like I need to, you know, say my last farewells to Mr. Finckelstein.

KATHRYN: Yeah. The rest of them can get their faces eaten off by zombies, but I am gonna miss Dad.

RANDALL: He was a great man. In his way.

KATHRYN: I just wish he'd loved us.

RANDALL: Yeah, *right*.

Beat.

KATHRYN: What do you mean, "Yeah, right"?

RANDALL: He loved you like crazy! All of you!

KATHRYN: Um… Have you been paying attention here?

RANDALL: Dude, it was obvious! All the stuff he did for you guys?

KATHRYN: What stuff?

RANDALL: Everything! The friggin'—!

KATHRYN: The friggin' what?

RANDALL: I don't know, the hikes, the camping trips, the dance classes, the talent shows, the fun runs, the cookouts, the sleepovers, the Parent-Teacher Organization fundraisers! Come on!

KATHRYN: I hated that stuff. I mean like, all of it.

RANDALL: Whatever! It's how he showed you his love!

Beat.

KATHRYN: Huh. Somehow it didn't mean anything, though. We didn't believe it. Why didn't we believe it?

RANDALL: Maybe you didn't want to for some reason.

KATHRYN: But why not?

RANDALL: Beats me. People are strange. But I'll tell you this: down in the basement? I found boxes, and I mean like, *boxes* of all your girlhood stuff. All three of you. Scrapbooks he put together. Every last little stupid doodle on a piece of junk mail. Every last cheap-ass certificate for "Runner Up." Friggin' 4th Grade book reports for cryin' out loud! He even wrote these little notes saying what each thing meant. It was like a museum. Or a church. Yes, he loved you. Case closed. So shut up about it already. Jesus!

KATHRYN: Wow.

Beat.

RANDALL: Oh: and there's also this… *(Pulls a manilla envelope out of his pocket)*

KATHRYN: What's that?

RANDALL: Maybe you should open it.

He hands her the packet, exits. She opens it, pulls out a thick sheaf of papers.

KATHRYN: *(Reading)* "Dear Julia, dear children. Being a family was not exactly our strong suit. In fact, we sucked. I acknowledge my part in that. As you can see, though, I've tried to set things right. The awful house you all hated has now been devoured by the frack-void along with my biological person, which I know was loathsome to you all. So there's that. But also, as the enclosed documents will make clear, I've designated you all equally my heirs. I had to do it that way because, like I said, we're not actually related. So Julia: you can now have as many new kitchens as you want. Enjoy! And I mean that sincerely. Kristin, Karen, Kathryn, your respective trust funds await the plundering. My advice, though: spend it on something you love. Not *like*, not *want*, not *need*, but *love*. That's the thing. Life's too short for all the other bullshit. Take it from me. *Adiós* and *l'Chaim*. Dad."

She looks up, smiles—maybe for the first time.
   Slow fade.
   Sound of Bub playing some bad-ass turn-of-the-century old-time fiddle.

About the Author

John Crutchfield, born in Austin, Texas, raised in Boone, North Carolina, and educated at the University of North Carolina (Chapel Hill) and at Cornell University, is a writer, performer, and teacher. His poems, essays, translations, and reviews have appeared in a variety of literary and cultural journals, including *Shenandoah, Seneca Review, Southern Review, Southern Poetry Review, Appalachian Journal, Zone 3, Berfrois, Newfound,* and oldtime-central.com. His plays have frequently premiered in Asheville, NC, and been produced in small regional theatres and at The New York International Fringe Festival, where he won an Outstanding Solo Performance award for The Songs of Robert, his one-man verse play with music, directed by Steven Samuels. He also designs and directs for the stage, and has served as Associate Artistic Director of The Sublime Theater & Press since its founding in 2018. At present, he teaches German at the University of North Carolina at Asheville and works freelance as a literary translator and editor.

www.ingramcontent.com/pod-product-compliance
Lightning Source LLC
Chambersburg PA
CBHW060408130526
44592CB00046B/740